Growth Mindset

Prayer Journal

THIS JOURNAL BELONGS TO:

Dedicated to my late Grand Aunt (Auntie Winnie) who prayed for me day and night.

Table of contents

Introduction

Growth Mindset Prayer Journal

Purpose of the Journal

Why You Should Pray

Reasons to Pray

What the Bible Says About Prayer

Key Biblical Teachings on Prayer

General Growth Mindset Prayers

Prayers for Schools and Educators

Prayers for Relationships

Prayers for Family and Friends

I know that sometimes we cannot find the words to say and for that reason I created this prayer journal for you! Remember that you can call on God anytime, anywhere and as much as you need. He is Omnipotent, Omniscient and Omnipresent.

In this journal , spaces were created for you to write your personal prayers but if you can not find the words at the moment, there are some here for you.

I decided to create this journal to help you cultivate a growth mindset while developing your prayer life. My late Grand Aunt always emphasized the importance of prayer. She always said "Mi love yuh and mi pray fi yuh day an nite" . (I love you and I pray for you everyday and every night).

I encourage you to pray day and night.

-Symonette Hibbert-

Here are a few reasons why you should pray:

1. **Connection with God** : Prayer fosters a personal relationship with God, allowing you to express your thoughts, feelings, and needs.

2. **Peace and Comfort**: Engaging in prayer can provide a sense of peace and comfort during challenging times, helping reduce anxiety and stress.

3. **Guidance and Wisdom:** Many people seek divine guidance through prayer, which can lead to greater clarity and understanding in decision-making.

4. **Community and Support**: Praying with others can strengthen community bonds and provide mutual support.

5. **Gratitude and Reflection:** Prayer encourages gratitude, helping individuals to reflect on their blessings and cultivate a positive mindset.

What the Bible Says About Prayer

1. **Communication with God:** The Bible emphasizes prayer as a means of communicating with God. In Philippians 4:6-7, it encourages us to present our requests to God, promising us peace in return.

2. **Faith and Trust:** Mark 11:24 states that whatever you ask in prayer, believe that you have received it, and it will be yours, highlighting the importance of faith.

3. **Persistence:** Luke 18:1 teaches the importance of persistent prayer, illustrating that one should always pray and not give up.

4. **Confession and Forgiveness:** James 5:16 indicates that prayer can bring healing and forgiveness, encouraging believers to confess their sins to one another and pray for each other.

5. **Intercession:** The Bible also speaks of intercessory prayer, where one prays on behalf of others (1 Timothy 2:1).

6. **Model of Prayer:** Jesus provided a model for prayer in the Lord's Prayer (Matthew 6:9-13), emphasizing reverence, dependence, and a focus on God's will.

Growth Mindset Prayer

Heavenly Father ,

I come before You with a grateful heart. Thank You for the gift of life and the chance to grow a little more each day. Please help me to see challenges not as roadblocks but as opportunities to become stronger and wiser. When I stumble, remind me that failure is not the end , it is a chance to learn and try again.

Fill me with resilience and courage Lord, so I can keep going even when things feel hard. Help me celebrate every bit of progress, no matter how small, and find joy in the journey of learning and becoming better.

As Your Word says in Philippians 4:13: "I can do all things through Christ who strengthens me." Please help me to lean on Your wisdom and strength, knowing that with You by my side, I can face anything.

Keep my thoughts positive and my heart open to new possibilities. Teach me to reflect Your love in all I do, so I can inspire and uplift those around me as we grow together.

Thank You for being my constant source of love, strength, and support. Thank you for all that you have done, all that you are doing and all that you are about to do . Amen.

My personal prayer

_____

_____

_____

_____

_____

_____

_____

_____

_____

_____

_____

_____

_____

_____

_____

_____

_____

Therefore I tell you, whatever you ask for in prayer, believe that you
have received it, and it will be yours. - Mark 11:24

Growth Mindset Prayer for My Children

Heavenly Father,

Thank You for the precious gift of my children. Parenting is not always easy, but I know You are here to guide me through it all. Please give me the wisdom and patience I need to nurture their hearts and minds with love.

Remind me of what you said in your word that "I can do all things through Christ who strengthens me" (Philippians 4:13). I want my kids to believe this with all their hearts . Remind them Lord that with Your strength, they can face any challenge and rise above it. Help me to celebrate their efforts, not just their achievements, and to show them that mistakes and setbacks are just stepping stones to growth. Remind me to speak words that uplift them and reflect Your promises, like the one in Jeremiah 29:11, where You declare that You have plans to prosper them and give them hope for the future.

Teach me how to create a home where they feel safe to try new things, dream big, and even fail, knowing they are loved unconditionally. Help them understand the truth of Romans 8:28: "In all things, You work for the good of those who love You." I want them to trust in Your purpose for their lives, even when things feel uncertain.

Thank You for the privilege of being their parent. Please help me reflect Your love and belief in their potential every single day. Thank you for all that you have done, all that you are doing and all that you are about to do . Amen.

My personal prayer

_____

_____

_____

_____

_____

_____

_____

_____

_____

_____

_____

_____

_____

_____

_____

_____

Therefore I tell you, whatever you ask for in prayer, believe that you
have received it, and it will be yours. - Mark 11:24

Growth Mindset Prayer for the School Year

Almighty God ,

I come before you with hope, excitement, and a little nervousness. Thank You for the opportunity to learn, grow, and discover my potential. Please walk with me every step of the way, guiding my heart and mind toward success.

Help me see challenges not as roadblocks, but as chances to grow stronger and wiser. When I make mistakes, remind me that they are part of the learning process and not something to fear. Give me the courage to keep trying, even when things feel tough, and the strength to believe in myself as You believe in me.

Your Word reminds me in Jeremiah 29:11 that You have "plans to prosper me and give me hope and a future." Help me trust in those plans when things do not go as I expect. Let me approach each day with an open mind, ready to learn, and a grateful heart, ready to celebrate both the victories and the lessons learned through setbacks.

Give me kindness to share with others, patience when I feel frustrated, and perseverance to keep moving forward. Help me build friendships that uplift me and focus on becoming the best version of myself.

Thank You for being my constant support and guide throughout this school year. I trust that You are working everything for my good, just as Romans 8:28 says. Thank you for all that you have done, all that you are doing and all that you are about to do . Amen.

My personal prayer

_____
_____
_____
_____
_____
_____
_____
_____
_____
_____
_____
_____
_____
_____
_____
_____
_____
_____

Therefore I tell you, whatever you ask for in prayer, believe that you have received it, and it will be yours. - Mark 11:24

Prayer for Teachers Throughout the School Year

Heavenly Father,

Thank You for the gift of teaching and the privilege of guiding my students. As I go through this school year, I ask for Your strength and wisdom each day. Help me approach every moment with patience, kindness, and a heart open to learning alongside my students.

When challenges arise, remind me that they are opportunities for growth for me , and for my students. Help me see their potential, even when they can not see it themselves, and give me the words to encourage and uplift them.

Lord, let my classroom be a place where curiosity thrives, where mistakes are embraced as part of the journey, and where every child feels safe, valued, and supported. Teach me to celebrate small victories and to show grace during tough times.

Guide my thoughts and actions so that I can model resilience, perseverance, and a love for learning. Remind me of Philippians 4:13: that says "I can do all things through Christ who strengthens me," and let this truth carry me through the busy, tiring, or overwhelming days.

Thank You for walking with me every step of this journey. May my efforts leave a lasting impact on my students' hearts and minds, shaping them for a future filled with hope and purpose. Thank you for all that you have done, all that you are doing and all that you are about to do . Amen.

My personal prayer

_____

_____

_____

_____

_____

_____

_____

_____

_____

_____

_____

_____

_____

_____

_____

_____

_____

Therefore I tell you, whatever you ask for in prayer, believe that you
have received it, and it will be yours. - Mark 11:24

Principal's Prayer for Growth

Most Righteous and Heavenly Father ,

Give us the courage to face obstacles with faith, the resilience to persevere, and the humility to learn from our mistakes. Teach us to celebrate every effort, no matter how small, and remind us that true growth takes time, patience, and determination.

Help me foster a school environment where curiosity flourishes, where every individual feels valued, and where both students and staff are encouraged to reach their full potential. Let our journey together be one of discovery, learning, and transformation ,not just academically, but in our character and faith as well.

As Your Word declares: "I can do all things through Christ who strengthens me." (Philippians 4:13). May this promise be the foundation of our efforts, giving us the confidence to trust in Your strength in every moment.

Thank You for the privilege of leading this amazing community. May we continue to grow together, supporting one another and glorifying You in all that we do. Thank You for all You have done, all You are doing, and all You are about to do in our lives.

Amen.

My personal prayer

_____

_____

_____

_____

_____

_____

_____

_____

_____

_____

_____

_____

_____

_____

_____

_____

_____

Therefore I tell you, whatever you ask for in prayer, believe that you
have received it, and it will be yours. - Mark 11:24

Growth Mindset Prayer for My Friend

Dear Lord,

Today, I lift up my friend to You. Give (Name) the strength and courage he/she needs to face life's challenges. Help him/her to see every obstacle as a chance to grow, and remind him/her of Your promise in Philippians 4:13: "I can do all things through Christ who strengthens me."

When things do not go as planned, help him/her see setbacks not as failures, but as stepping stones to something greater. Fill his/her heart with resilience and remind him/her of James 1:2 ,that the trials he/she faces will build perseverance, making him/her stronger, wiser, and complete.

Lord, surround my friend with encouragement and positivity. When doubt creeps in, remind him/her of his/her potential and Your promise in Jeremiah 29:11: "For I know the plans I have for you, plans to prosper you and not to harm you, plans to give you hope and a future."

I pray that each day he/she wakes up with a heart ready to grow, learn, and become the best version of himself/herself. Thank You for blessing me with his/her friendship. May we continue to support, encourage, and uplift one another as we walk together in Your love and grace.

Thank you for all that you have done, all that you are doing and all that you are about to do . Amen.

My personal prayer

_____
_____
_____
_____
_____
_____
_____
_____
_____
_____
_____
_____
_____
_____
_____
_____

Therefore I tell you, whatever you ask for in prayer, believe that you
have received it, and it will be yours. - Mark 11:24

A Growth Mindset Prayer for a Mom

Heavenly Father,

Thank You for the amazing gift of my mom. I am so grateful for her love, wisdom, and the way she touches everyone around her. Today, I pray that You help her embrace each challenge as an opportunity to grow and learn. Lord, renew her mind and perspective, reminding her that with You, all things are possible as you said in Matthew 19:26. Please give her peace of mind, especially when things feel overwhelming.

Help her see setbacks not as failures, but as chances to become stronger and wiser. Let her hold onto the truth of Philippians 4:13, "I can do all things through Christ who strengthens me," and may she find courage and encouragement in Your Word.

Surround her with love and support, and inspire her to chase her dreams with passion. Remind her that Your guidance will be with her every step of the way.

Fill her heart with hope and joy, and let her be a light to others, showing Your love and grace. I pray she continues to grow in faith, wisdom, and strength, trusting in Your perfect plan for her life.

Thank you for all that you have done, all that you are doing and all that you are about to do .Amen.

My personal prayer

Therefore I tell you, whatever you ask for in prayer, believe that you have received it, and it will be yours. - Mark 11:24

22

Growth Mindset Prayer for My Dad

Heavenly Father ,

Today, I lift up my dad to You. I pray that You bless him with a growth mindset, helping him to see every challenge as an opportunity to grow and learn. In moments of struggle, remind him of Philippians 4:13, "I can do all things through Christ who strengthens me." May he always find strength in You and the courage to embrace new experiences, even when they feel uncertain.

Help him to see setbacks not as failures but as stepping stones on his journey. Let him remember Proverbs 24:16, "For a righteous man falls seven times and rises again," and give him the resilience to rise with renewed determination, no matter what comes his way. Fill his heart with the joy of perseverance, knowing that every effort counts.

Surround him with love and encouragement, and let him feel Your presence guiding him through each step. When fear or doubt creep in, remind him of Your promise in Isaiah 41:10: "Do not fear, for I am with you; do not be dismayed, for I am your God." Help him to remember that he is never alone in his struggles.

I pray that my dad continues to embrace growth in every season of life. Help him to celebrate even the smallest progress and inspire those around him with his example. Thank You for the incredible gift of my dad and for the lessons he teaches me every day.

Thank you for all that you have done, all that you are doing and all that you are about to do . Amen.

My personal prayer

_____

_____

_____

_____

_____

_____

_____

_____

_____

_____

_____

_____

_____

_____

_____

_____

_____

Therefore I tell you, whatever you ask for in prayer, believe that you have received it, and it will be yours. - Mark 11:24

Growth Mindset Prayer for My Sister

Almighty Father,

I come before You today with a heart full of gratitude for the gift of my sister. Thank You for the unique gifts and talents You have placed within her. I ask that You help her embrace a growth mindset, believing in her potential and the endless possibilities that You have set before her.

Lord, help her to see every challenge as an opportunity to grow. Remind her of Philippians 4:13, "I can do all things through Christ who strengthens me." May she always lean on Your strength as she faces obstacles, trusting that You are with her every step of the way.

Grant her the courage to step outside of her comfort zone, knowing that each effort she makes brings her closer to becoming who You created her to be. May she renew her thoughts each day, focusing on the positive and embracing the possibilities that lie ahead. Fill her heart with resilience, so that when she stumbles, she rises again with even greater determination.

Lord, surround her with encouragement and support from those who love her. May she find joy in the process of learning and growing, celebrating each small victory along the way. Help her to always remember that she is fearfully and wonderfully made (Psalm 139:14) and that her journey is uniquely hers.

I pray for peace in her heart as she pursues her dreams, knowing that You have a future filled with hope for her (Jeremiah 29:11). Thank You for the amazing sister that she is. I believe in her, and I trust in Your guiding hand over her life.

Thank you for all that you have done, all that you are doing and all that you are about to do . Amen.

My personal prayer

_____

_____

_____

_____

_____

_____

_____

_____

_____

_____

_____

_____

_____

_____

_____

_____

_____

Therefore I tell you, whatever you ask for in prayer, believe that you
have received it, and it will be yours. - Mark 11:24

Growth Mindset Prayer for My Brother

Oh Heavenly Father,

I come before You today with a heart full of love and gratitude for my brother. I ask for Your guidance and strength to fill his heart and mind. Please help him embrace every challenge with courage, knowing that each obstacle is an opportunity for growth and transformation.

Lord, remind him of the truth in Philippians 4:13, "I can do all things through Christ who strengthens me." May he always trust in Your power as he faces difficulties, believing in his ability to learn and persevere through all things, big and small.

Grant him the wisdom to grow in knowledge and understanding, as Proverbs 1:5 says, "Let the wise hear and increase in learning." Inspire him to see each experience, even failures, as steps toward success, knowing that each lesson brings him closer to who You have created him to be.

 May he strive to grow personally and spiritually, always keeping his eyes on the path You have laid out for him. Fill his heart with resilience, Lord. When he faces setbacks, help him to rise each time, stronger and wiser than before. Surround him with encouragement and support, and let him feel Your presence guiding him along the way.

Thank You, Father, for the wonderful plans You have for him ,plans to prosper him and not to harm him, plans to give him a future filled with hope (Jeremiah 29:11).

Thank you for all that you have done, all that you are doing and all that you are about to do . Amen.

My personal prayer

_____

_____

_____

_____

_____

_____

_____

_____

_____

_____

_____

_____

_____

_____

_____

_____

_____

_____

Therefore I tell you, whatever you ask for in prayer, believe that you
have received it, and it will be yours. - Mark 11:24

Growth Mindset Prayer for My Grandmother

Almighty Father,

I come before You today with a heart full of gratitude for my grandmother. Thank You for the wisdom she shares, the strength she carries, and the countless ways she has touched our lives. Lord, I lift her up to You now, asking that You fill her with a spirit of growth, renewal, and joy.

Grant her the courage to step out of her comfort zone, knowing that You are guiding her every step of the way. As You remind us in Isaiah 40:31, "Those who hope in the Lord will renew their strength." May she experience that renewal daily, finding joy in each new chapter, each new lesson, and each new moment.

Lord, fill her heart with gratitude for the beauty in every day. As 1 Thessalonians 5:16-18 encourages us, "Rejoice always, pray continually, give thanks in all circumstances." May her heart overflow with thankfulness, radiating Your goodness and inspiring those around her to do the same.

I pray that my grandmother will always see her life as a testament to Your grace. Help her to recognize that age is not a limitation but an opportunity to reflect on the richness of wisdom gained over the years. As Proverbs 16:31 says, "Gray hair is a crown of splendor; it is attained in the way of righteousness." May she wear her years with pride, knowing they reflect a life lived in faith and love.

Lord, as she continues her journey, fill her with hope and excitement for all that lies ahead. Give her peace in knowing that each step she takes is part of Your perfect plan for her. Thank you for all that you have done, all that you are doing and all that you are about to do . Amen.

My personal prayer

_____

_____

_____

_____

_____

_____

_____

_____

_____

_____

_____

_____

_____

_____

_____

_____

_____

Therefore I tell you, whatever you ask for in prayer, believe that you
have received it, and it will be yours. - Mark 11:24

Growth Mindset Prayer for My Grandfather

Dear Heavenly Father,

I come before You with a heart full of gratitude for my grandfather. Thank You for the love, wisdom, and strength he has shared with me and our family throughout his life. Lord, I lift him up to You today, asking that You fill him with Your peace and grace, and bless him with a renewed spirit of growth and possibility.

Father, remind him of the powerful truth in Isaiah 40:31: "But those who hope in the Lord will renew their strength. They will soar on wings like eagles; they will run and not grow weary, they will walk and not be faint." May Your strength be his foundation, helping him navigate each new day with resilience and courage, knowing that You are with him always.

Grant him a heart open to learning and growth. Help him to see every challenge as an opportunity to deepen his understanding and expand his horizons.

Lord, fill his heart with hope and trust in Your plans for him. Help him to recognize that his journey is far from over, and that age is a gift, full of experiences, opportunities, and potential. May he find strength in the knowledge that You are always guiding him, and that with You, all things are possible.

Thank You for the blessing of my grandfather's life. I pray that he continues to embrace every season with a heart of growth, courage, and hope. May he feel Your love surrounding him, and may his life be a testimony to Your goodness. Thank you for all that you have done, all that you are doing and all that you are about to do. Amen.

My personal prayer

_____

_____

_____

_____

_____

_____

_____

_____

_____

_____

_____

_____

_____

_____

_____

_____

_____

Therefore I tell you, whatever you ask for in prayer, believe that you have received it, and it will be yours. - Mark 11:24

Growth Mindset Prayer for My Stepmom

Almighty God,

I come before You today with a heart full of gratitude for my stepmom. Thank You for the blessing of her presence in my life and for the love and care she shows. I ask that You fill her heart with Your peace, strength, and a renewed spirit of growth.

Lord, help her embrace every challenge she faces as an opportunity to grow closer to You. Remind her of Your promise in Philippians 4:13, "I can do all things through Christ who strengthens me." May she lean on Your strength in times of uncertainty and find confidence in Your guiding hand.

Help her to trust You fully, as Proverbs 3:5-6 reminds us: "Trust in the Lord with all your heart, and lean not on your own understanding; in all your ways acknowledge Him, and He shall direct your paths." Let her feel Your presence in every decision, knowing that You are guiding her every step of the way.

Fill her heart with courage, resilience, and hope. When she faces setbacks, help her see them as opportunities to learn and grow stronger. May her mind and spirit be open to Your transformation, bringing new perspectives and possibilities.

Thank You, Lord, for the unique journey You have given my stepmom. Surround her with Your love, wisdom, and encouragement as she walks this path of growth and change. Thank you for all that you have done, all that you are doing and all that you are about to do . Amen.

My personal prayer

_____
_____
_____
_____
_____
_____
_____
_____
_____
_____
_____
_____
_____
_____
_____
_____
_____

Therefore I tell you, whatever you ask for in prayer, believe that you have received it, and it will be yours. - Mark 11:24

Growth Mindset Prayer for My Stepdad

Dear Lord,

I come before You with a heart full of gratitude for my stepdad. Thank You for the love and guidance he brings into my life. I ask that You bless him with a spirit of growth and resilience.

Help him to embrace challenges as opportunities for growth, just as Your Word teaches us in James 1:2-4: "Consider it pure joy, my brothers and sisters, whenever you face trials of many kinds, because you know that the testing of your faith produces perseverance." May he find strength in perseverance and joy in the journey.

Lord, grant him the courage to step out of his comfort zone, knowing that with You, all things are possible (Matthew 19:26). Let him remember that every setback is a setup for a comeback and that he is never alone in his struggles.

Surround him with encouragement and support, and help him to see the potential within himself. Let him recognize that he is fearfully and wonderfully made (Psalm 139:14) and that his growth is a testament to Your grace.

Thank You Lord for the incredible man he is and the journey he is on. May he continue to inspire others as he embraces a growth mindset, fueled by Your love and wisdom.

Thank you for all that you have done, all that you are doing and all that you are about to do . Amen.

My personal prayer

_____
_____
_____
_____
_____
_____
_____
_____
_____
_____
_____
_____
_____
_____
_____
_____
_____

Therefore I tell you, whatever you ask for in prayer, believe that you
have received it, and it will be yours. - Mark 11:24

BE ENCOURAGED

There are going to be days when you feel overwhelmed . Here are few reminders :

- EMBRACE THE JOURNEY OF GROWTH, KNOWING THAT EVERY CHALLENGE TEACHES YOU SOMETHING VALUABLE, EVERY SETBACK PREPARES YOU FOR SUCCESS, AND EVERY SMALL STEP FORWARD IS A TESTAMENT TO YOUR STRENGTH. AS ROMANS 12:2 REMINDS US, "BE TRANSFORMED BY THE RENEWING OF YOUR MIND."

- YOUR POTENTIAL HAS NO LIMITS WHEN YOU TRUST IN THE POWER OF YET. EACH NEW DAY OFFERS AN OPPORTUNITY TO GROW, REMINDING US THAT WITH GOD, ALL THINGS ARE POSSIBLE, AS STATED IN MATTHEW 19:26.

- GROWTH BEGINS WHEN YOU STEP OUTSIDE YOUR COMFORT ZONE AND LEAN INTO FAITH. TRUST THE PROCESS, FOR PERSEVERANCE SHAPES THE PERSON YOU ARE BECOMING. JAMES 1:4 ENCOURAGES US, "LET PERSEVERANCE FINISH ITS WORK SO THAT YOU MAY BE MATURE AND COMPLETE, NOT LACKING ANYTHING."

- TRUE STRENGTH COMES FROM COMBINING FAITH WITH A GROWTH MINDSET. BELIEVE IN YOUR ABILITY TO OVERCOME CHALLENGES, LEARN FROM EVERY EXPERIENCE, AND THRIVE. PHILIPPIANS 4:13 ASSURES US, "I CAN DO ALL THINGS THROUGH CHRIST WHO STRENGTHENS ME."

My personal prayer

_____
_____
_____
_____
_____
_____
_____
_____
_____
_____
_____
_____
_____
_____
_____
_____
_____
_____

Therefore I tell you, whatever you ask for in prayer, believe that you
have received it, and it will be yours. - Mark 11:24

Growth Mindset Prayer for a Family Member

Dear Heavenly Father,

I come before You with a heart full of hope for (Name). I pray that You bless him/her with a growth mindset, empowering him/her to embrace challenges and see failures as opportunities for growth.

Help him/her remember Philippians 4:13: "I can do all things through Christ who strengthens me." May he/she find strength in Your presence, knowing that with You, he/she is capable of overcoming any obstacle.

Lord, instill in him/her a spirit of perseverance, as your word says in James 1:2-4: "Consider it pure joy, my brothers and sisters, whenever you face trials of many kinds, because you know that the testing of your faith produces perseverance." Let him/her find joy in his/her journey, knowing that each step brings him/her closer to Your purpose.

Surround him/her with Your love and support, reminding him/her of Romans 12:2: "Do not be conformed to this world, but be transformed by the renewal of your mind." Help him/her renew his/her thoughts and embrace the possibilities that lie ahead.

Thank You, Lord, for the incredible potential You have placed within him/her. May he/she feel Your guidance and encouragement as he/she strives to grow.

Thank your for all that you have done, all that you are doing and all that you are about to do . Amen.

My personal prayer

_____

_____

_____

_____

_____

_____

_____

_____

_____

_____

_____

_____

_____

_____

_____

_____

_____

Therefore I tell you, whatever you ask for in prayer, believe that you
have received it, and it will be yours. - Mark 11:24

Growth Mindset Prayer about forgiveness

Heavenly Father,

I come to You today with a heavy heart, seeking Your guidance and wisdom. My relationship with (Name) has been challenging, and I find myself struggling with conflicting emotions. Lord, I ask for Your divine perspective to see him/her as You do, with compassion and understanding.

Your Word teaches us in Luke 6:28 to "Bless those who curse you, pray for those who mistreat you." Father, I confess this is difficult for me, but it is my desire to follow Your teachings. Please help me with these negative feelings that I am experiencing.

I recognize that (Name) may be facing his/her own struggles. I lift him/her up to You, asking for Your healing touch in his/her life. Almighty God, I acknowledge my own need for Your grace and guidance. Please help me release this burden of bitterness that weighs so heavily on my spirit.

 Grant me the strength to be kind and forgiving, even when it feels impossible. I humbly ask for Your peace for (Name), for myself, and for all involved. Help me grow through this experience rather than becoming hardened by it. Give me the courage to embrace change and to view circumstances through the lens of Your love.

Lord You know my heart and so today I leave this situation in your hands . Thank you for all that you have done, all that you are doing and all that you are about to do . Amen.

My personal prayer

_____

_____

_____

_____

_____

_____

_____

_____

_____

_____

_____

_____

_____

_____

_____

_____

Therefore I tell you, whatever you ask for in prayer, believe that you
have received it, and it will be yours. - Mark 11:24

Growth Mindset Prayer for My Partner (Current)

Most Gracious and Heavenly Father ,

I come to You with a grateful heart, thanking You for the special bond I share with my partner. I lift him/her up to You Lord, asking that You guide him/her and fill his/her heart and mind with Your strength.

Please help my partner grow in ways that show Your love and purpose. Let him/her remember Your promise in Jeremiah 29:11: "For I know the plans I have for you," You say, "plans to prosper you and not to harm you, plans to give you hope and a future."

Help him/her trust in Your plan, Lord. Show him/her that even when things are hard, it is all part of the journey You have set out for him/her. Help my partner see that even when he/she stumbles, it is a chance to learn and grow. Your word tells us in Proverbs 24:16, "The righteous fall seven times and rise again." Give him/her the strength to get back up each time, knowing he/she can overcome any challenge with Your help.

Lord, build in him/her a spirit of resilience and determination. Remind him/her of the truth in Philippians 4:13, that he/she "can do all things through Christ who strengthens me." When doubts creep in, let him/her lean on You Mighty God .Wrap him/her in Your love through encouragement and support.

Use me Lord, to be a beacon of Your love and positivity in his/her life. Let him/her feel Your presence always, knowing he/she is never alone on this journey. Thank You Father for the amazing person my partner is and all the potential You have placed within him/her. As we follow the paths You have set before us, may our bond grow stronger in Your love. Thank You for all that You have done, all that You are doing, and all that You are about to do. Amen.

My personal prayer

_____

_____

_____

_____

_____

_____

_____

_____

_____

_____

_____

_____

_____

_____

_____

_____

_____

Therefore I tell you, whatever you ask for in prayer, believe that you
have received it, and it will be yours. - Mark 11:24

Growth Mindset Prayer for My Partner (Future)

Dear Heavenly Father,

I come to You today with a heart full of hope and love, thinking of the partner You have in store for me. Though I have not met him/her yet, I trust in Your perfect timing and plan. As Your word says in Jeremiah 29:11, "For I know the plans I have for you," declares the Lord, "plans to prosper you and not to harm you, plans to give you hope and a future."

Lord, I pray for my future partner's growth and well-being. Please nurture in him/her a mindset that embraces challenges and sees opportunities in every situation. Help him/her to view his/her journey through Your eyes, recognizing that You have wonderful plans for his/her life.

When he/she faces setbacks, remind him/her that stumbling is part of learning. Give him/her the courage to get back up, dust himself/herself off, and try again. Let him/her know it is okay to make mistakes , that is how we grow and become stronger. May he/she always remember Philippians 4:13, which tells us, "I can do all things through Christ who strengthens me."

I pray that You surround him/her with people who encourage and support his/her growth. I pray he/she has friends and mentors who believe in him/her and cheer him/her on, even when he/she doubts himself/herself.

Lord, help me to grow too, so that when we meet I can be a supportive and loving partner. Guide us both to become the best versions of ourselves, ready to face life's adventures together. Remind us that through Christ, we can overcome any challenge that comes our way.

Thank You for the amazing person You are preparing for me. I am excited to meet him/her when you decide that the time is right.

I know You have plans to prosper us and give us hope, I trust in Your perfect plan for our lives and future together. Thank you for all that you have done, all that you are doing and all that you are about to do. Amen.

My personal prayer

_____

_____

_____

_____

_____

_____

_____

_____

_____

_____

_____

_____

_____

_____

_____

_____

_____

Therefore I tell you, whatever you ask for in prayer, believe that you have received it, and it will be yours. - Mark 11:24

Growth Mindset Prayer for Difficult Times

Dear Most loving God,

In this tough time, I find myself struggling and in need of Your comfort. Lord, life feels heavy right now, and I am not sure how to move forward but I know that You are with me, even when things are hard.

Mighty Father, help me see this challenge as a chance to grow stronger in my faith and as a person. When I am feeling scared or doubtful, remind me of Your words in Isaiah 41:10: "So do not fear, for I am with you; do not be dismayed, for I am your God. I will strengthen you and help you; I will uphold you with my righteous right hand."

Please give me the strength to keep going, even when I want to give up. Help me to be patient with myself and to learn from my mistakes Almighty God .

Heavenly Father, as Your Word in James 1:2-4 reminds me, trials are opportunities to grow and build perseverance. Help me embrace challenges with joy, trusting that You are shaping me into who I am meant to be. Teach me to see obstacles as lessons and trust Your process, growing in faith and strength.

I trust that You have a plan for me, even if I can not see it right now. Thank You for being with me always and for giving me the strength to keep going. As Philippians 4:13 reminds me, "I can do all this through Christ who strengthens me." Lord I put my life in your hands today. Please lead me and guide me.

Thank you for all that you have done, all that you are doing and all that you are about to do. Amen.

My personal prayer

_____

_____

_____

_____

_____

_____

_____

_____

_____

_____

_____

_____

_____

_____

_____

_____

_____

Therefore I tell you, whatever you ask for in prayer, believe that you have received it, and it will be yours. - Mark 11:24

Growth Mindset Graduation Prayer

Dear Heavenly Father,

I come before You today with a heart full of gratitude. Thank You for guiding me to this incredible moment in my life. As I stand here today, I am grateful for this journey.

Lord, I am grateful for every experience that shaped me , the late nights cramming for exams, the friendships that kept me going, and even the failures that taught me resilience. I know that every step, every struggle, and every triumph has been part of Your plan for me.

Father, as I look towards the future, I am asking for Your courage to face whatever comes my way. Help me remember that You are always by my side, even when the path ahead seems unclear.

God, I pray that You will nurture in me a passion for growth. When I face challenges , and I know I will, help me see them not as barriers, but as opportunities to learn and become a better version of myself. When I stumble, give me the strength to get back up, knowing that with You all things are possible.

Lord, keep my mind open and my spirit teachable. Help me to always be eager to learn, to ask questions, and to seek wisdom , both from You and from the people You place in my life. Let me never become so proud that I think I have all the answers.

Father, I need Your guidance as I make decisions about my future. Give me discernment to choose paths that honor You and allow me to use the gifts You have given me to make a positive difference in the world.

And Lord, in those moments when doubt creeps in , when I wonder if I am good enough or if I can really make it , help me remember Your promises. Remind me that You have plans to prosper me, to give me hope and a future as your words says in Jeremiah 29:11. Let that truth sink deep into my heart and give me the confidence to keep pressing on. Thank You for bringing me to this moment, and I entrust my future into Your loving hands. May my life be a testament to Your grace and goodness. Thank you for all that you have done, all that you are doing and all that you are about to do. Amen.

My personal prayer

_____

_____

_____

_____

_____

_____

_____

_____

_____

_____

_____

_____

_____

_____

_____

_____

Therefore I tell you, whatever you ask for in prayer, believe that you have received it, and it will be yours. - Mark 11:24

Growth Mindset Prayer for Embracing Opportunities

Dear Heavenly Father,

I come to You with a mix of excitement and nerves. Thank You for the opportunities You have placed before me. When I feel overwhelmed, remind me of Your promise in Jeremiah 29:11: "For I know the plans I have for you," declares the Lord, "plans to prosper you and not to harm you, plans to give you hope and a future."

Give me courage, Lord, to step into the unknown. When I am afraid, help me to remember 2 Timothy 1:7: "For God has not given us a spirit of fear, but of power and of love and of a sound mind."

Let me see challenges as opportunities to grow, not roadblocks. Open my eyes to the possibilities around me. Grant me wisdom in my decisions, as James 1:5 encourages: "If any of you lacks wisdom, you should ask God, who gives generously to all without finding fault, and it will be given to you."

In everything, let me reflect Your love. I may not know where these opportunities will lead, but I trust in Your guidance, as Proverbs 3:5-6 teaches: "Trust in the Lord with all your heart and lean not on your own understanding; but in all your ways acknowledge him, and he shall direct thy path."

Thank You for believing in me and for walking with me on this journey. Thank you for all that you have done, all that you are doing and all that you are about to do. Amen.

My personal prayer

_____

_____

_____

_____

_____

_____

_____

_____

_____

_____

_____

_____

_____

_____

_____

_____

_____

Therefore I tell you, whatever you ask for in prayer, believe that you
have received it, and it will be yours. - Mark 11:24

Growth Mindset Prayer for a Job Interview

Heavenly Father,

As I prepare for this job interview, I come before You with gratitude and humility. Thank You for the opportunity to showcase the talents and skills You have blessed me with. I trust that You are with me in every step of this journey, guiding my path according to Your will.

Lord, remind me of Your promise in Jeremiah 29:11: "For I know the plans I have for you," declares the Lord, "plans to prosper you and not to harm you, plans to give you hope and a future." Help me to trust in Your plan for my life, knowing that what is meant for me will never pass me by.

Grant me confidence, as it says in Philippians 4:13, "I can do all things through Christ who strengthens me." Give me the courage to speak clearly and with conviction, allowing my true self to shine through. Help me to remember that my worth is not determined by this interview, but by who I am in You.

Help me to replace fear with faith, knowing that You are my constant support. Lord, as I walk into this interview, let Your peace calm my mind so that I may respond thoughtfully and confidently.

Regardless of the outcome, help me to embrace this experience as an opportunity for growth. May I trust that, as it says in Romans 8:28, "And we know that in all things God works for the good of those who love Him, who have been called according to His purpose." May this interview be another step toward the purpose You have prepared for me.

Lord in Your hands, I place my hopes, my fears, and this opportunity. I trust that whatever happens, You have a plan far greater than I could imagine. Thank you for all that you have done, all that you are doing and all that you are about to do. Amen.

My personal prayer

_____

_____

_____

_____

_____

_____

_____

_____

_____

_____

_____

_____

_____

_____

_____

_____

Therefore I tell you, whatever you ask for in prayer, believe that you have received it, and it will be yours. - Mark 11:24

Growth Mindset Prayer for Grief

Heavenly Father,

My heart is so heavy right now. This grief feels like more than I can bear. I need You Lord. I need Your comfort and Your strength. When the pain is too much, help me remember that You are right here with me. You see my tears, You know my heartache. Hold me close Father because I need You more than ever right now. Remind me of Your Words in Psalm 34:18, "The Lord is close to the brokenhearted and saves those who are crushed in spirit." Let me feel Your presence, especially when I feel most alone.

Sometimes I wonder if I will ever feel okay again. In those moments, remind me that this pain will not last forever. Help me to hold onto hope, even when it is hard. Give me the strength to keep going, to take it one day at a time.

God, I do not understand why this happened but I am trusting that You can bring something good out of even this. Help me to grow through this grief, not just endure it. Remind me of Your promise in Romans 8:28, "And we know that in all things God works for the good of those who love him, who have been called according to his purpose."

Give me the courage to face each day. When I feel weak, be my strength. When I feel lost, please guide me. Lord when I feel alone, remind me that You are always by my side. Help me to be patient with myself as I navigate this journey of grief.

Almighty Father, show me how to honor the memory of what I have lost while still moving forward. Help me to find moments of peace and joy, no matter how small, in the midst of my sorrow.

Thank You for Your love that never leaves me, even in my darkest moments. Thank you guiding me through this moment dear Father. Thank you for all that you have done, all that you are doing and all that you are about to do. Amen.

My personal prayer

_____

_____

_____

_____

_____

_____

_____

_____

_____

_____

_____

_____

_____

_____

_____

_____

_____

Therefore I tell you, whatever you ask for in prayer, believe that you have received it, and it will be yours. - Mark 11:24

Growth Mindset Prayer for Love Life

Heavenly Father,

I come before You with a heart open to love, seeking Your wisdom and guidance. Thank You for the gift of love and the beauty it brings into our lives. As I navigate my journey in relationships, I ask for Your blessing to lead me in the right direction and to fill my heart with patience, grace and understanding.

Lord, remind me of Your words in 1 Corinthians 13:4-7: "Love is patient, love is kind. It does not envy, it does not boast, it is not proud. It does not dishonor others, it is not self-seeking, it is not easily angered, it keeps no record of wrongs. Love does not delight in evil but rejoices with the truth. It always protects, always trusts, always hopes, always perseveres."

Help me to embrace these qualities in my own heart, that I may love others as You have loved me. When I face uncertainty in my love life, remind me of Proverbs 3:5-6: "Trust in the Lord with all your heart and lean not on your own understanding; in all your ways acknowledge Him, and He shall direct thy path."

Give me the courage to trust Your timing and to be patient in the unfolding of Your plan for my relationship. In moments of disappointment or heartache, help me find strength in Psalm 147:3: "He heals the brokenhearted and binds up their wounds." Heal any past wounds that might hold me back, and guide me toward a love that reflects Your grace and goodness.

Help me to trust that every connection, every joy, and even every heartache is shaping me into the person You want me to be. May I love fearlessly, with a heart that is open and ready to give and receive love, knowing that with You by my side, I am never alone. I surrender my love life into Your hands, trusting that You will guide me toward relationships that honor You, bring joy to my heart, and draw me closer to the purpose You have for my life.

Thank you for all that you have done, all that you are doing and all that you are about to do. Amen.

My personal prayer

_____

_____

_____

_____

_____

_____

_____

_____

_____

_____

_____

_____

_____

_____

_____

_____

Therefore I tell you, whatever you ask for in prayer, believe that you have received it, and it will be yours. - Mark 11:24

Growth Mindset Prayer for the Spirit of Discernment

Heavenly Father,

I come before You with a humble heart, seeking the gift of discernment. In this world full of choices, voices, and distractions, I need Your wisdom to guide me. Thank You for always being my source of light and truth. I ask that You sharpen my spirit to discern what is right, what is true, and what aligns with Your will for my life.

I ask for wisdom Lord, to see clearly and to understand what You want me to do in every situation. Help me to trust in Your guidance as it says in Proverbs 3:5-6: "Trust in the Lord with all your heart and lean not on your own understanding; in all your ways acknowledge Him, and He shall direct thy path." Grant me the courage to lean not on my limited understanding but to trust in Your infinite wisdom.

When I am uncertain, remind me of Philippians 1:9-10: "And this is my prayer: that your love may abound more and more in knowledge and depth of insight, so that you may be able to discern what is best and may be pure and blameless for the day of Christ." Help my love for You to grow deeper, so that my discernment may be sharp and true, allowing me to choose what is best in every situation.

Give me the strength to remain steadfast in my faith, especially when the world's temptations and confusion surround me. Teach me to test the spirits, to listen carefully to Your voice, and to distinguish between what is of You and what is not. Lord, help me to live with a growth mindset, believing that even in my mistakes, You are teaching me to discern better.

Renew my mind daily so that I may walk in alignment with Your will. I surrender my thoughts, decisions, and actions to You, trusting that You will guide me. Let me walk in Your light, confident that You are leading me every step of the way. Thank you for all that you have done, all that you are doing and all that you are about to do . Amen.

My personal prayer

_____

_____

_____

_____

_____

_____

_____

_____

_____

_____

_____

_____

_____

_____

_____

_____

_____

Therefore I tell you, whatever you ask for in prayer, believe that you have received it, and it will be yours. - Mark 11:24

Growth Mindset Prayer for Consistency

Dear Heavenly Father,

Lord, I come before You today with a heart longing to cultivate consistency. I thank You for every opportunity You have given me to pursue my dreams, build good habits, and strive toward the purpose You have set for my life. Lord, I recognize that without consistency, I cannot fully realize the potential You have placed within me.

Grant me the perseverance to keep going even when the journey feels long or difficult. Help me to trust in the harvest that You have promised will come from my consistent efforts. When I am tempted to quit or grow complacent, remind me that You are always with me. Help me to stand firm in my commitments, knowing that with each small step forward, I am making progress that honors You.

Father, when I feel discouraged or lack motivation, remind me of Hebrews 12:11 "No discipline seems pleasant at the time, but painful. Later on, however, it produces a harvest of righteousness and peace for those who have been trained by it."

Help me to remember that the discipline of consistency, though challenging, will ultimately bring peace and growth into my life. Grant me the wisdom to discern what truly matters, that I may focus my energy on what brings lasting fruit. Let me trust in Proverbs 16:3 . "Commit to the Lord whatever you do, and He will establish your plans." Help me to commit my goals, plans, and daily actions to You, so that You may establish them according to Your will. Lord, fill me with the spirit of perseverance and a growth mindset, so that I may not just start strong but also finish well.

Let my journey be a testament to Your faithfulness, for with You, I know that all things are possible. Thank you for all that you have done, all that you are doing and all that you are about to do . Amen.

My personal prayer

_____

_____

_____

_____

_____

_____

_____

_____

_____

_____

_____

_____

_____

_____

_____

_____

_____

Therefore I tell you, whatever you ask for in prayer, believe that you
have received it, and it will be yours. - Mark 11:24

Growth Mindset Prayer to Strengthen My Faith

Dear Heavenly Father,

I come before You today with a humble heart, longing to grow deeper in my faith. I thank You for Your unfailing love, Your guidance, and Your endless patience with me. Lord, I desire a faith that is strong, unwavering, and rooted firmly in You, no matter the storms that come my way.

Lord, remind me of Your promise in Hebrews 11:1: "Now faith is the substance of things hoped for, the evidence of things not seen" . Help me to trust in You even when I cannot see the full picture, knowing that You are always working things out for my good.

When doubts and fears cloud my mind, remind me of 2 Corinthians 5:7: "For we walk by faith, not by sight." Grant me the courage to step forward with confidence, not because I understand everything, but because I trust in Your wisdom and plan.

In moments of weakness, strengthen me with Your words in Isaiah 40:31: "But those who hope in the Lord will renew their strength. They will soar on wings like eagles; they will run and not grow weary, they will walk and not be faint." Renew my spirit, Lord, so that I may rise above my challenges with the strength and resilience that comes from You alone.

Father, when my faith feels small, remind me of Matthew 17:20 "If you have faith as small as a mustard seed, you can say to this mountain, 'Move from here to there,' and it will move. Nothing will be impossible for you." Teach me that even a small amount of faith can accomplish great things when I place it in Your hands.

Cultivate in me a growth mindset, so that I may see every trial as an opportunity to strengthen my faith and draw closer to You. Help me embrace the challenges before me, knowing that they are refining me and drawing me nearer to You.

Lord, may my faith be not just in words but in action, reflecting Your love and grace to those around me. Let me be a beacon of hope, showing others the power of trusting in You. Thank you for all that you have done, all that you are doing and all that you are about to do.
Amen.

My personal prayer

_____
_____
_____
_____
_____
_____
_____
_____
_____
_____
_____
_____
_____
_____
_____
_____
_____

Therefore I tell you, whatever you ask for in prayer, believe that you
have received it, and it will be yours. - Mark 11:24

Growth Mindset Prayer for When I Struggle to Pray

Dear Heavenly Father,

I come before you at this time because I am feeling lost, weary, and unable to find the words to pray. My heart feels heavy, and my spirit is tired, yet I trust in Your constant presence. Thank You for always listening, even when my heart struggles to speak. I ask for Your comfort and strength to carry me through this difficult time. Lord, I hold on to Your promise in Romans 8:26, that the Spirit helps us in our weakness and intercedes for us when words fail. Even in my silence, I trust that Your Spirit is praying on my behalf with a depth I cannot comprehend.

Lord, when doubt clouds my mind and I feel distant from You, guide me to the place of refuge promised in Psalm 61:2, where I can be led to the rock that is higher than I. Remind me that no matter how far I feel, You are always near, ready to catch me and hold me. When I am unsure of what to say, let my simple cry of "Help me, Lord" be enough, knowing that You understand my heart better than I do.

Strengthen my faith, Lord, and help me to remember the wisdom of Philippians 4:6-7, to not be anxious but to bring my concerns to You with thanksgiving, trusting in Your peace that surpasses all understanding. Let me rest in the knowledge that Your love for me is unconditional, and even in my brokenness, You are there, holding me when I feel too weak to pray.

Thank You for all You have done, all You are doing, and all You are about to do in my life. Amen.

My personal prayer

_____

_____

_____

_____

_____

_____

_____

_____

_____

_____

_____

_____

_____

_____

_____

_____

_____

_____

Therefore I tell you, whatever you ask for in prayer, believe that you have received it, and it will be yours. - Mark 11:24

My personal prayer

_____

_____

_____

_____

_____

_____

_____

_____

_____

_____

_____

_____

_____

_____

_____

_____

_____

Therefore I tell you, whatever you ask for in prayer, believe that you have received it, and it will be yours. - Mark 11:24

My personal prayer

_____

_____

_____

_____

_____

_____

_____

_____

_____

_____

_____

_____

_____

_____

_____

_____

Therefore I tell you, whatever you ask for in prayer, believe that you
have received it, and it will be yours. - Mark 11:24

My personal prayer

Therefore I tell you, whatever you ask for in prayer, believe that you have received it, and it will be yours. - Mark 11:24

69

My personal prayer

_____

_____

_____

_____

_____

_____

_____

_____

_____

_____

_____

_____

_____

_____

_____

_____

_____

Therefore I tell you, whatever you ask for in prayer, believe that you
have received it, and it will be yours. - Mark 11:24

My personal prayer

_____

_____

_____

_____

_____

_____

_____

_____

_____

_____

_____

_____

_____

_____

_____

_____

Therefore I tell you, whatever you ask for in prayer, believe that you have received it, and it will be yours. - Mark 11:24

My personal prayer

_____

_____

_____

_____

_____

_____

_____

_____

_____

_____

_____

_____

_____

_____

_____

Therefore I tell you, whatever you ask for in prayer, believe that you have received it, and it will be yours. - Mark 11:24

My personal prayer

_____

_____

_____

_____

_____

_____

_____

_____

_____

_____

_____

_____

_____

_____

_____

Therefore I tell you, whatever you ask for in prayer, believe that you have received it, and it will be yours. - Mark 11:24

My personal prayer

_____

_____

_____

_____

_____

_____

_____

_____

_____

_____

_____

_____

_____

_____

_____

_____

_____

Therefore I tell you, whatever you ask for in prayer, believe that you
have received it, and it will be yours. - Mark 11:24

My personal prayer

_____

_____

_____

_____

_____

_____

_____

_____

_____

_____

_____

_____

_____

_____

_____

_____

Therefore I tell you, whatever you ask for in prayer, believe that you have received it, and it will be yours. - Mark 11:24

My personal prayer

_____

_____

_____

_____

_____

_____

_____

_____

_____

_____

_____

_____

_____

_____

_____

_____

Therefore I tell you, whatever you ask for in prayer, believe that you have received it, and it will be yours. - Mark 11:24

My personal prayer

Therefore I tell you, whatever you ask for in prayer, believe that you have received it, and it will be yours. - Mark 11:24

My personal prayer

_____

_____

_____

_____

_____

_____

_____

_____

_____

_____

_____

_____

_____

_____

_____

_____

_____

Therefore I tell you, whatever you ask for in prayer, believe that you have received it, and it will be yours. - Mark 11:24

My personal prayer

Therefore I tell you, whatever you ask for in prayer, believe that you have received it, and it will be yours. - Mark 11:24

My personal prayer

_____

_____

_____

_____

_____

_____

_____

_____

_____

_____

_____

_____

_____

_____

_____

_____

_____

Therefore I tell you, whatever you ask for in prayer, believe that you have received it, and it will be yours. - Mark 11:24

My personal prayer

_____

_____

_____

_____

_____

_____

_____

_____

_____

_____

_____

_____

_____

_____

_____

_____

_____

Therefore I tell you, whatever you ask for in prayer, believe that you
have received it, and it will be yours. - Mark 11:24

My personal prayer

_____

_____

_____

_____

_____

_____

_____

_____

_____

_____

_____

_____

_____

_____

_____

_____

Therefore I tell you, whatever you ask for in prayer, believe that you have received it, and it will be yours. - Mark 11:24

My personal prayer

_____

_____

_____

_____

_____

_____

_____

_____

_____

_____

_____

_____

_____

_____

_____

Therefore I tell you, whatever you ask for in prayer, believe that you have received it, and it will be yours. - Mark 11:24

www.ingramcontent.com/pod-product-compliance
Lightning Source LLC
Chambersburg PA
CBHW041616120626
46551CB00003B/473